A Commu
Guid

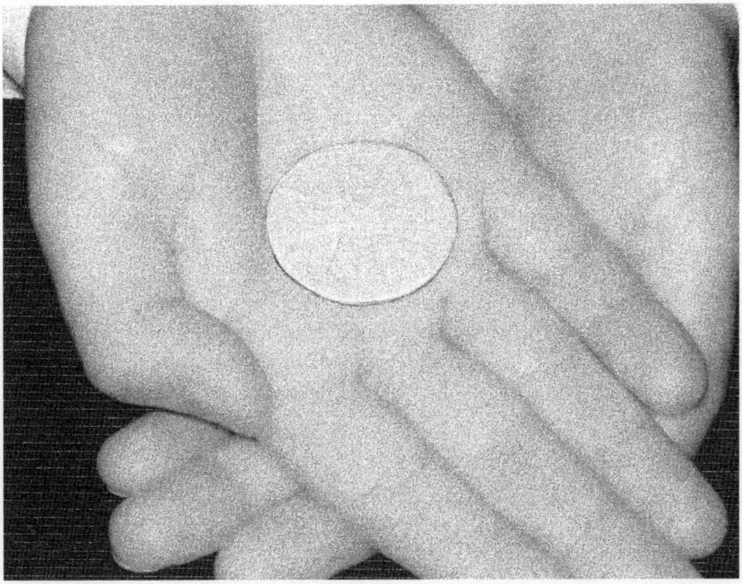

Robert Beaken

FOREWORD

by Bishop Edwin Barnes.

Here is a manual for communicants which will encourage and help them as they settle into the life of the worshipping community. It is thoroughly practical and answers the questions that many of us should like to ask but do not, feeling we might be thought silly for not knowing. The section at the end with suggestions for helping us prepare to receive Holy Communion and for giving thanks afterwards is especially worthwhile. *A Communicant's Guide* is just the thing for godparents or parishes to give to the newly confirmed; and indeed just the thing to help all of us renew and deepen our devotion.

+ Edwin Barnes

A COMMUNICANT'S GUIDE

Holy Communion, the Eucharist, the Mass: all these names are used by Anglicans for the sacrament instituted by Jesus Christ during the Last Supper which is the central act of Christian worship and which has been celebrated by Christians for twenty centuries ever since.

The Eucharist contains many layers of meaning and significance. For a start, it is a sacred meal during which Christians are united in fellowship with the rest of the congregation at that particular service and also with all other Christians throughout the world and throughout history. The Eucharist is also a celebration of Christ's presence and a means whereby he reaches out to us. The Lord is present in three ways during every Eucharist: he is present in the congregation gathered together in his name; he is present in the proclamation of his Gospel; and he is present under the veils of bread and wine following their consecration in the eucharistic prayer. In his presence here (often called the Real Presence) the Lord makes real his promise made at the Last Supper that *'this is my body'* and *'this is my blood.'* We meet Christ here and recognise him as surely as the disciples recognised him at Emmaus (St Luke, chapter 24, verses 13 to 35).

The Eucharist also ties in with the events of Holy Week, so that in a sense when we gather at Christ's altar we find ourselves sitting amongst the disciples at the Last Supper, standing at the foot of the cross with Mary and John on Good Friday, and also peering into the tomb with Peter, John and the women on Easter Day and finding it empty, for Christ had risen.

The Eucharist is above all a celebration of God's love for each of us. Christ comes to us in this sacrament so that we may enjoy and be helped by his loving presence, his grace and his strength. We should place the Eucharist at the very heart of our Christian lives, together with regular private prayer, Bible reading, and the stewardship of our time and money in the service of God.

PREPARATION.

At its best, the Anglican spiritual tradition has always valued careful preparation before receiving Holy Communion, prayerful participation in the service, and thanksgiving afterwards. This little work aims to try to help us do all three of these thing more effectively.

We might start by thinking about the frequency of Communion. I would suggest that we should try to receive Holy Communion every Sunday and on the major holy days during the Christian year. Many Anglicans also find it helpful to come to a midweek Eucharist as well. I suggest you should work out some rule, i.e. a pattern of attendance which you may exceed but will not fall below, and then **stick to it.**

If you are being prepared for Confirmation you might be tempted to think that you are unworthy to receive Holy Communion. Well, of course, we are **all** unworthy! But that is the whole point of the Eucharist: Christ comes to us in love, knowing that we are each a great mixture of good and bad, and he seeks to draw us closer to him and to help us through Holy Communion. We, for our part, are to respond with faith. Part of our preparation on Saturday before receiving Holy Communion on Sunday must be finding time for quiet prayer during which we can review the week that is drawing to a close, thank God for the good things and honestly own up to our sins: the times we have let Him down or offended the men and women who are made in His image. We should try to recall these sins on Sunday morning when we say the prayer of confession during the Eucharist so that it is meaningful to us. Sometimes we find that there are some sins which plague our conscience and however much we pray we cannot seem to get rid of them. In these circumstances the Anglican spiritual tradition suggests that we might make a special confession to God in the presence of one of His priests (also known as the sacrament of Reconciliation) and receive absolution. If you think this may be the case with you, pray to God and ask Him to guide you. Any priest will be more than happy to talk to you in confidence and answer your questions about confession.

Another important part of preparation is to try to read the collect (special prayer for the day) and the readings from the Bible on Saturday. Look them up in your Lectionary (again, any priest or member of the congregation will be happy to explain the book to you) and spend a moment or two thinking about them. If you have your own book, it is an excellent idea to take it to church with you and follow the readings as they are read.

The new Church of England *Common Worship* service book provides a suggested form of preparation to be used at home before coming to church. This begins with the hymn *'Come Holy Ghost',* which is a prayer that the Holy Spirit will guide us. It then suggests that we read the Ten Commandments or some other texts such as the Beatitudes or Christ's summary of the Law to help us reflect and confess our sins. We might want to add other prayers to this, such as those printed at the end of this booklet.

A further preparation before receiving Holy Communion is fasting (not eating or drinking anything). We should somehow feel that it was not right if we were to receive the Body and Blood of Christ when we were full up after a heavy meal and since ancient times Christians have fasted from Midnight and made Holy Communion the first thing they ate and drank in the morning. In recent years the Roman Catholic Church has modified this to an hour before Holy Communion and many Anglicans have followed their example. In either case, fasting is a useful reminder to us that what we eat and drink in Holy Communion is sacred and should be treated and received as such. Medicines, pills and tablets, however, are not included in this and may be taken before receiving Holy Communion.

BODY LANGUAGE.

In everyday life we use body language to show respect and love. The same is true in church: down the centuries a rich language of postures, actions and gestures has arisen whereby Christians express their faith with their bodies as well as with their thoughts and words. Sometimes, when our attention wanders during the service, body language can bring it back and help us focus on what we are doing. You will need to think carefully about how much body language to use and it is important to understand its significance.

Standing.

We stand for much of the service - in past centuries we should have stood for nearly all of it, as Christians still do in the Orthodox Church - and although the congregation now sits for some of the service, we still stand for some of the most important parts such as the entrance of the clergy, the *kyries* (Lord, have mercy, etc.), the *Gloria* (Glory to God in the highest, etc.), the Gospel, the Creed (We believe in one God, etc.), the first part of the eucharistic prayer, and in some churches to receive Holy Communion.

Kneeling.

We kneel to pray and in many churches to receive Holy Communion. If you are able to kneel, it is much better to do so than to crouch forward on the pew or chair: we kneel in adoration and to remind ourselves that God is very big and we are very small (an idea we frequently forget once we have left the church!).

Bowing.

Since the seventeenth century Anglicans have bowed their heads slightly when the holy name of *Jesus* is mentioned during the service as a sign of love and respect for their Lord. The further custom arose over the centuries of bowing more deeply during the reference to the Incarnation in the Creed - *'he became incarnate from the Holy Spirit and the Virgin Mary and was made man',* or also *'by the power of the Holy Spirit he became incarnate of the Virgin Mary and was made man*' - as a sign of faith and wonder at God's saving work for humanity.

The sign of the cross.

The cross is *the* symbol of Jesus Christ. As well as depicting the cross in our churches and in Christian art, we also make the sign of the cross (with the palm of the right hand turned inwards: forehead, tummy, left shoulder, right shoulder) during the service as a reminder that Christ loved us so much he offered his life on the cross to God the Father as a sacrifice to take away our sins. As a general rule, you should make the sign of the cross whenever the priest does so during the service. You may also wish to do so before receiving Holy Communion and when you begin and end your private prayers. Some Anglicans make the sign of the cross using their right thumbs upon their forehead, mouth and heart when the Gospel reading is announced: this is a prayer that their thoughts, words and emotions may be guided by the Gospel.

Genuflection.

This literally means *'to bend the knee'* and it is a gesture of love towards Jesus Christ in his Real Presence in the bread and wine once they have been consecrated into his sacramental Body and Blood. To genuflect, stand upright and then kneel, going down on the right knee and bringing it level with the left foot, then stand upright again. Christians may genuflect when going to receive Holy Communion and when passing the place in church where the sacrament is reserved for the sick and dying.

THE SUNDAY EUCHARIST.

Having made your preparation on Saturday, get to church in good time on Sunday morning and spend the few minutes before the service starts in silent prayer, finishing your preparation and getting ready to meet Christ in the Eucharist. Avoid the temptation to talk: a talkative communicant is often an unprepared communicant. Of course there are times when it is important to say something, perhaps to help a stranger who is unfamiliar with the service book or to greet someone who has bravely come to church after a long illness or a bereavement, but in most cases conversation is best saved until afterwards. Many communicants with hectic lives value a moment of quiet prayer in church before the service begins and we should not like to think that we had inadvertently disturbed their prayers by our conversation.

Once the service begins try to give it your full attention. When the prayer of confession is said, remember all the sins of the past week which you recalled during your preparation and ask God to forgive you. During the readings from the Bible listen carefully as they are spiritual food. Listen carefully to the sermon: even the worst sermon contains some good point!

During the intercessions try to visualise the people and places being prayed for. When the names of the sick and the departed are read out, add silently the names of any other people you can remember who are not mentioned.

The Peace springs from Jesus' teaching in St Matthew, chapter five, verses 23 - 24:

> *So if you are offering your gift at the altar, and there remember that your brother has something against you, leave your gift there before the altar and go; first be reconciled to your brother, and then come and offer your gift.*

In our terms this means that we should not receive Holy Communion if we are in a rage with someone, nor if we are bearing grudges and refusing to forgive or be reconciled. God forgives us many sins each day and we must forgive others as He has forgiven us.

At the offertory the bread and wine are carried up to the priest who prepares them upon the altar ready for the eucharistic prayer (also known as the prayer of consecration). As you see them carried up and offered to God in the offertory prayers, offer your whole life afresh to Him and pray that this Holy Communion will lead you ever closer to His great heart of love. Pay particular attention during the eucharistic prayer. As the priest repeats the words of Jesus Christ from the Last Supper whilst holding the bread and the chalice of wine, they are transformed by the Holy Spirit into the sacramental Body and Blood of Christ. The priest may elevate (lift up) the consecrated host (the bread, now the Body of Christ) and the chalice (now containing the Blood of Christ): as he does so, you might like to look at them, make the sign of the cross and say silently each time *'my Lord and my God.'*

Receiving Holy Communion.

You will probably be invited to leave your seat and go to receive Holy Communion by a churchwarden or sidesman or woman. Otherwise use your judgement about when to leave your seat and go up. You might like to genuflect as you step into the aisle as a sign of your love towards Jesus in the sacrament. Try not to gaze around (difficult if you are taking children up with you for a blessing) and avoid conversation. Use these last moments to prepare yourself for Holy Communion by telling Jesus silently that you love him and perhaps silently repeating the words *'Come into my heart Lord Jesus, there is room in my heart for thee.'*

In many churches Holy Communion is received kneeling at a rail in front of the altar. Wait until you see a space and then go and kneel down. As the priest draws near you might wish to make the sign of the cross. You should then hold out your hands with the right palm uppermost on top of the left palm. The priest will say *'The Body of Christ'* to which you should reply *'Amen.'* The priest will then place the host on your palm: lift the host up with both hands to your mouth and consume it immediately. Some Anglicans follow the continental custom of receiving the host on the tongue: after you have said *'Amen'* open your mouth and the priest will place the host on your tongue. This method is particularly helpful to parents using both hands to hold babies whilst kneeling at the altar rail.

Another priest, a deacon or a lay minister of the Eucharist will follow administering the Blood of Christ from the chalice. He or she will say *'The Blood of Christ'* to which you again reply *'Amen.'* The rim of the chalice will be placed against your lips and you should take a sip: many people find it helpful gently to guide the chalice to their lips with their hands but care should be taken that nothing is spilt. It will be a great help to the person administering the chalice if you kneel upright and your mouth is visible.

You should remain kneeling until the communicant next to you has received from the chalice and then stand up. You might wish to genuflect again before making your way back to your seat, where you should kneel in silent prayer until all of the sacrament has been consumed. Pray that Christ whose Body and Blood you have received will guide and strengthen you in the week ahead and help you to serve others.

In many churches and at large diocesan services Holy Communion is often administered standing, an older custom which has much to commend it. Leave your seat as before and make your way to the altar or communion point. Receive the host in the usual way and then go to the person administering the chalice standing nearby. It is probably best not to genuflect in order to avoid accidents but you might like to bow instead. Return to your seat as before.

In some churches and religious communities Holy Communion is administered in a circle. You will either be invited to come up and stand around the altar either at the offertory, so you remain standing throughout the eucharistic prayer, or during the *Agnus Dei* (Lamb of God, etc.). The host and chalice may be brought to you by the priest or you may pass them around the circle and communicate each other, in which case you should turn to face the person on your right who will administer the host to you. When you have received, firmly take hold of the ciborium (special container for the host), turn to the person on your left, lift up one of the hosts and say *'The Body of Christ.'* When the communicant has said *'Amen'* administer the sacrament by placing it in the palm or on the tongue. Then give the communicant the ciborium. Turn back to the person on your right and now receive the Blood of Christ from him or her. Once you have received, carefully take hold of the chalice in your right hand and the purificator (linen cloth for cleansing the chalice) in your left hand. Wipe with the purificator the part of the rim of the chalice which your lips touched. Turn again to the communicant on your left and say *'The Blood of Christ.'* When the communicant has said *'Amen'* guide the chalice to his or her lips, taking very great care. Once the communicant has received, carefully hand over the chalice and purificator. When all have received Holy Communion, return to your seat.

THANKSGIVING.

Just as we should say 'thank you' to someone who had invited us to a meal or a party, we ought also to thank Jesus Christ for Holy Communion. When you have returned to your seat in the church after receiving Holy Communion, kneel down and silently thank Jesus. Join in a hymn if one is sung and listen to the post-communion prayer. As you go home - and when you are tempted to sin later in the day - say to yourself *"I have Christ inside me, I must try to live up to that."* Before going to bed, find time for private prayer: reflect on the day that is past. See how much of the sermon you can remember, and again thank Christ for feeding you with his Body and Blood. You might find it helpful to say a hymn from the Holy Communion section of the hymn book if you have a copy.

WHAT NEXT?

You will recall that when Jesus Christ instituted the Eucharist during the Last Supper he also washed the feet of the twelve disciples and said to them:

> *Do you know what I have done to you? You call me Teacher and Lord; and you are right, for so I am. If I then, your Lord and Teacher, have washed your feet, you also ought to wash one another's feet. For I have given you an example, that you also should do as I have done to you.* (St John, 13. 12b-16).

Christ's gift to us of his Real Presence in the sacrament is very precious but it is a means to an end and not an end in itself. Christ feeds us with his Body and Blood in order that we may be nourished during our earthly pilgrimage and may begin to be transformed into the sort of Christian men and women he has always planned that we shall be. We, for our part, must co-operate with the Holy Spirit. This means we must listen to God when we pray and seek His will for our lives. We must try to do something about those parts of our lives which we know are not up to the teachings of Christ in the New Testament. We must also follow his example of service to one another. It would be a terrible thing if we received the Body and Blood of Christ in Holy Communion and then walked out of church and began mistreating our fellow men and women or ignoring their needs. Christ comes to us in the Eucharist to meet our needs: we must go out to others and try to be of help or comfort to them. Who do you know who is in need or trouble and whom you might be able to help? We should do so with no thought of reward and we should make a special effort to help those who are awkward or not particularly grateful. When *we* need help, we should accept it with good grace. In so far as we are able, we should also try to do something about the ways in which men, women and children are exploited. How do your Communions bear fruit?

NOTES.

If you have been unable to prepare before the Eucharist.

We all lead very hectic lives and have many family and work commitments. Sometimes - rarely, one hopes - there will be occasions when for good reasons the communicant will not find it possible to prepare before the Eucharist. In such circumstances, provided your conscience is clear, carry on as usual, receive Holy Communion and then make your preparation afterwards as part of your thanksgiving. After a bereavement, an illness or an operation it may be as much as we can do to get to church for the Eucharist and it may be very hard for us to concentrate our thoughts on preparation or thanksgiving. In these circumstances we should not worry too much and should allow other Christians to support us with their prayers.

If you get to church late on Sunday.

A previous generation would have said very firmly that if you get to church after the Gospel has been read you should not receive Holy Communion. As a general rule I should say that this is still a good discipline if you are late because of laziness. There may be situations, however, where providing you have made your preparation the night before, you might still receive Holy Communion if you are late for a good reason. The sort of thing I have in mind is when you are delayed because your baby is sick as you are leaving the house and needs changing, or the car will not start or breaks down and you have to walk to church, or you do someone a good turn on Sunday morning before the Eucharist and are held up. In these circumstances not only would it probably be right to receive the sacrament but one might imagine Jesus positively encouraging it. It would not be right, however, to receive Holy Communion if you are habitually late and have made no spiritual preparation beforehand.

Accidents.

It sometimes happens that the Blood of Christ may be spilt on someone's shirt or blouse during Holy Communion. Such accidents can be upsetting but they are only accidents and Christ is not offended by them. The only lesson to be learnt is to be more careful the next time. A previous generation would have said that the shirt or blouse should be burned, but shirts and blouses are expensive and may not easily be spared. One has to take a sensible line about such accidents and I would suggest that the best thing to do is to wash the garment in cold water and then throw the water over consecrated ground (a churchyard) or if this is not possible over a garden. The garment should then be washed in the usual way. Sometimes communicants can be distressed if the part of the host becomes stuck in their teeth: do not worry, it will dissolve. Concentrate on enjoying the rest of the Eucharist.

Nuptial and Requiem Masses.

A Nuptial Mass is a celebration of the Eucharist as part of a wedding service. Receiving Holy Communion alongside someone you love can be a wonderful bond between you both and it is good to bring Christ into your marriage through the Eucharist and receive his sacramental grace from the very start.

A Requiem Mass is a celebration of the Eucharist at a funeral or on another occasion when the Eucharist is offered as one great prayer of commendation of the soul of whoever has died into the hands of our heavenly Father. It is not an attempt to bribe God to modify His judgement about someone: that would be blasphemous. Rather, we pray for our loved ones in death as we did in life, and, as Archbishop William Temple once put it, we claim the privilege of uniting our love for the departed with God's.

It is sometimes said the Nuptial and Requiem Masses ought not to be celebrated if they might embarrass those members of the congregation at the wedding or funeral who are not churchgoers. Such thoughtfulness is commendable but I believe is misplaced: what matters most is the faith of the bride and groom or of the departed Christian. Your parish priest will be happy to discuss the details of the service with you and is only anxious that the wedding or funeral will help you. If you would like a Requiem after you have died, please write it down.

Reservation of the Blessed Sacrament.

In many churches and all cathedrals the sacrament is reserved for the sick and dying. If you cannot get to church and would like Holy Communion, please ask for the sacrament to be brought to you: your parish priest will be only too pleased to be asked. He will conduct a very simple service in your house or beside your bed and give you Holy Communion. If you are seriously ill or are about to have an operation, you might like to ask to be anointed with special holy oil to give you strength and peace from God: again your parish priest will be only too pleased to discuss this with you.

The Blessed Sacrament is usually reserved is a special cupboard on an altar (called a tabernacle) or set into a wall (called an aumbry) in church and a candle is burnt in a white glass container (or a red container in Roman Catholic churches) to indicate the place. One of the unlooked-for gifts of God is that the chapel or part of the church where the sacrament is reserved comes to have a special stillness and peace about it. When you visit a church or cathedral it is a good idea to spend a few moments in quiet prayer to Jesus in front of the reserved sacrament and enjoy the special sense of peace. When you go into a hospital, find time to pray in front of the reserved sacrament in the hospital chapel, pour out all your thoughts, worries or joys to the Lord and let him help and strengthen you.

AND FINALLY

When we begin to receive Holy Communion for the first few times after Confirmation it can be a very wonderful and uplifting experience. After a while we 'come down to earth again.' Not every celebration of the Eucharist can be an exhilarating spiritual experience, nor should we expect it to be.

God's sacramental grace, however, will be at work within us whether we are aware of it or not, and mostly we are not. Attending the Eucharist will become a matter of routine. A routine can be healthy but a rut is not. Just as we may take a person we love for granted, so we may also come to take the Eucharist for granted. From time to time we all need to ask ourselves whether this is the case? If it is, the answer may be that we need to give more time and thought to preparation and thanksgiving. There may perhaps be some unresolved sin in our lives which has grown up like a mist between us and God and which must be cleared away by repentance and confession. We may find it helpful to go on a quiet day or a retreat or perhaps to take part in a parish mission. Conversely, at the most unexpected times we may find ourselves powerfully and wonderfully conscious of the presence of Christ in the Eucharist.

Our understanding and appreciation of the Eucharist is bound to change as the years go by and we mature as Christians. Every celebration has the potential to be a life-changing encounter with Jesus Christ. Enjoy it.

PRAYERS OF PREPARATION AND THANKSGIVING.

Useful passages of Scripture.

St Matthew, chapter 26, verses 26 - 29. St Mark, chapter 14, verses 22- 25. St Luke, chapter 22, verses 14 - 23. St John, chapter 6, verses 35 - 59. St John, chapter 13, verses 1 - 17. 1 Corinthians, chapter 11, verses 23 - 29. Revelation, chapter 3, verse 20.

PREPARATION.

1 Almighty, everlasting God,
I draw near to the sacrament
of your only-begotten Son,
our Lord Jesus Christ.
I who am sick approach the physician of life.
I who am unclean come to the fountain of mercy;
blind, to the light of eternal brightness;
poor and needy, to the Lord of heaven and earth.
Therefore, I implore you, in your boundless mercy,
to heal my sickness, cleanse my defilement,
enlighten my blindness, enrich my poverty,
and cloth my nakedness.
Then shall I dare to receive the bread of angels,
the King of kings and Lord of lords,
with reverence and humility,
contrition and love,
purity and faith,
with the purpose and intention necessary
for the good of my soul.
Grant, I beseech you, that I may receive
not only the Body and Blood of the Lord,
but also the grace and power of the sacrament.
Most merciful God,
enable me so to receive the Body

of your only-begotten Son,
our Lord Jesus Christ,
which he took from the Virgin Mary,
that I may be found worthy
to be incorporated into his mystical Body,
and counted among his members.
Most loving Father,
grant that I may one day see face to face
your beloved Son, whom I now intend to receive
under the veil of the sacrament,
and who with you and the Holy Spirit,
lives and reigns for ever,
one God, world without end. Amen.

ST THOMAS AQUINAS.

2 I believe, O Lord, and confess
that you are truly the Christ,
the Son of the living God,
who came into the world to save sinners,
of whom I am the chief.
I also believe that this is your spotless Body
and precious Blood.
I therefore beseech you to have mercy upon me,
and to forgive me all my sins
committed in thought, word and deed;
willingly and unwillingly,
knowingly and unknowingly;
and make me fit to partake of your holy Mysteries,
for the remission of sins,
and for eternal life. Amen.

ST JOHN CHRYSOSTOM.

3 O blessed Saviour,
I, a poor unworthy sinner,
have an earnest longing to come to thy table;
but considering my many and grievous sins,
I tremble and fear to approach unto it.
I come therefore to thee,
the fountain of mercy,
hoping that thou wilt wash me;
I come to thee, the Good Samaritan,
hoping that thou wilt cleanse my wounds:
I open my grief, and discover my iniquities to thee;
I look upon my sins, great and grievous,
and thereupon tremble;
yet, beholding thy mercies great and plentiful,
I am therewith again refreshed.
Remember, O Lord,
how many pains and sorrows
thou didst sustain to expiate my sins.
I entreat thee therefore by them
to purge and purify me,
that I may be worthily incorporated into thy body,
which is thy Church,
and may also worthily receive this sacrament,
that so, together with thy whole Church,
I may give praise to thee everlastingly. Amen.

BISHOP LANCELOT ANDREWES.

4 Thanks be to thee,
O Lord Jesu Christ,
for all the cruel pains thou hast borne for me;
for all the many blessings thou hast won for me.
O holy Jesu,
most merciful redeemer,

friend and brother,
may I know thee more clearly,
love thee more dearly,
and follow thee more nearly. Amen.

ST RICHARD OF CHICHESTER.

5 Lord Jesus,
I love you,
help me to love you more,
and to love you
in those around me. Amen.

THANKSGIVING.

6 *Anima Christi.*
Soul of Christ, sanctify me,
body of Christ, save me,
blood of Christ, refresh me,
water from the side of Christ, wash me,
passion of Christ, strengthen me.
O good Jesus, hear me.
Within your wounds hide me.
Let me not be separated from you,
from the malicious enemy defend me,
in the hour of my death call me
and bid me come to you,
that with all your saints I may praise you,
for ever and ever. Amen.

7 Father of all, we give you thanks and praise,
that when we were still far off
you met us in your Son and brought us home.

Dying and living,
he declared your love,
gave us grace,
and opened the gate of glory.
May we who share Christ's body, live his risen life;
we who drink his cup, bring life to others;
we whom the Spirit lights, give light to the world.
Keep us firm in the hope that you have set before us,
so we and all your children shall be free,
and the whole earth live to praise your name;
through Christ our Lord. Amen.

1980 ALTERNATIVE SERVICE BOOK.

8 Glory be to thee, O Jesus,
my Lord and my God,
for thus feeding me
with thy most blessed body and blood.
O let thy heavenly food
transfuse new life and new vigour
into my soul,
and into the souls of all who communicate with me,
that our faith may daily increase;
that we may all grow more humble
and contrite for our sins;
that we may love thee,
and serve thee,
and delight in thee,
and praise thee more fervently,
more incessantly,
than ever we have done heretofore.
Amen.

BISHOP THOMAS KEN.

9 We adore thee, O God, and with our whole heart bless thee, who dost sustain and renew us with the communion of the most holy Body and Blood of our Saviour Jesus Christ, the utmost glory of thy love, the very seal of our redemption, the wonder of our souls; and we beseech thee, that he may abide in us, speaking grace and peace unto our lives, until we be possessed of everlasting life in him; to whom with thee and the Holy Ghost, one God, be glory and worship world without end. Amen.

ERIC MILNER-WHITE.

10 Teach us, good Lord,
to serve thee as thou deservest;
to give and not to count the cost;
to fight and not to heed the wounds;
to toil and not to look for rest;
to labour and not to seek for any reward,
save that of knowing we do thy will.
Who livest and reignest,
world without end. Amen.

ST IGNATIUS.

11 Blessed and praised be Jesus Christ
in the most holy sacrament.
Hosanna, hosanna, hosanna in excelsis.

ACKNOWLEDGEMENTS.

Photograph by Peter Collen

Scripture quotations are from *The Revised Standard Version of the Bible* copyright ©1946, 1952 and 1971 by the Division of Christian Education of the National Council of Churches in the USA. Used by permission. All Rights Reserved.
Prayer 1 from *The Weekday Missal* Collins, page 1285f.
Excerpts from *The Roman Missal* © 1973, International Committee on English in the Liturgy, Inc. All Rights Reserved.
Prayer 2 from *Catholic Prayers for the Church of England People*, W. Knott and Sons, 1936, page 139, rendered into contemporary English by the author.
Prayer 3 and 8 from Samuel Wilberforce (ed.) *Eucharistica*, R.and A.Sutterby, J.H. Parker, 1874, pages 57f and 100f.
Prayers 4, 6 (amended by the author), and 10 from *A Manual of Catholic Devotion for Members of the Church of England*, Church Literature Association, 1969, pages 10 and 167, and used by permission.
Prayer 7 from *The Alternative Service Book, 1980*, Clowes, S.P.C.K., Cambridge University Press, 1980, page 144.
The prayer taken from *The Alternative Service Book, 1980*, is copyright by The Central Board of Finance, 1980; The Archbishops' Council, 1999, and is reproduced by permission.
Prayer 9 from Eric Milner-White, *After the Third Collect*, A.R. Mowbray and Co., 1954, page 97, and is reproduced here by permission of Mowbray, an imprint of Continuum.

Print Management by shop4print